After Eden

After Eden

Harold J. Recinos

RESOURCE *Publications* · Eugene, Oregon

AFTER EDEN

Copyright © 2018 Harold J. Recinos. All rights reserved. Except for brief quotations in critical publications or reviews, no part of this book may be reproduced in any manner without prior written permission from the publisher. Write: Permissions, Wipf and Stock Publishers, 199 W. 8th Ave., Suite 3, Eugene, OR 97401.

Resource Publications
An Imprint of Wipf and Stock Publishers
199 W. 8th Ave., Suite 3
Eugene, OR 97401

www.wipfandstock.com

PAPERBACK ISBN: 978-1-5326-5462-6
HARDCOVER ISBN: 978-1-5326-5463-3
EBOOK ISBN: 978-1-5326-5464-0

Manufactured in the U.S.A.   07/24/18

Contents

The Crossing • 1
Shithole • 3
Color • 4
Rudy • 6
Lost Name • 7
The Apartment • 8
The Border • 9
The Scent • 11
The Storm • 13
The Sting • 14
The Garden • 16
The Painter • 17
Devotion • 19
The Substitute • 21
War Drums • 22
Waiting • 23
Bricks • 24
The Shore • 26
Resurrection • 27
Spanish Harlem • 28
Ivory Tower • 30
The Protest • 31
Factory Work • 32
The Raid • 34
The Spot • 36
Latino Heritage Month • 37
Prayer • 38
Look Here • 39
The Decay • 41

Imagine • 42
American Dream • 43
Faith • 44
Rise • 45
The Talk • 46
Fifth Avenue • 48
Daily Bread • 50
American Shore • 52
Stony the Road • 54
Ancient Shore • 56
Good Night • 58
Paradise • 59
The Maid • 61
The Stranger • 62
Missed • 63
The Room • 65
The Reach • 66
Morning Light • 68
Mi Barrio • 70
The North Side • 71
Sutherland • 73
Weep • 74
Enough Practice • 75
The Meditation • 76
Homeless • 77
The Kitchen • 79
Nevertheless • 81
Hit • 82
The Dark • 84

Old Streets • 85
Innocence • 86
Passing • 87
The Martyrs • 88
Affection • 90
Advent • 91
Letter to the White House • 92
Love • 94
The Garden • 95
The Bus Ride • 96
The Beach Day • 98
Thanksgiving • 100
The Migrant • 101
Faces • 102
Politics • 104
Simple • 105
Needle Park • 107
The Balm … • 109
Things • 110
Thin Walls • 112
The Library • 114
The Giver • 115
Wordless • 117
The Postman • 118
Departed • 120
Bridwell Library • 122
The Gift • 124
Saint Christopher • 126
The Park • 128
Witness • 129
A New Song • 131
The Season • 133
The Café • 134
Iron Cage • 136
The Stone • 138

War • 139
Work • 140
Bethlehem • 141
The Miracle • 143
Cathedral Steps • 144
Not Far • 145
Tax Reform • 150
Homeless • 151
Unto Us … • 153
Departure • 154
The Box • 155
Redemption • 157
The Infant • 158
Waiting • 159
The Rescue • 161
New Year • 163
The Bus • 165
The Sad Years • 167
Come • 168
The Priest • 169
Manna • 171
Snapshot • 173
Thought • 175
Martin • 176
Holy Spirit • 177
High Ground • 179
Dawn • 181
Passage • 183
No Safe Haven • 184
Get Out! • 186
The Border • 188
El Salvador • 190
Paradise • 192
Holy • 193
The Word • 194

Hold My Hand • 195
Dark Space • 197
Politics • 198

Romero • 200
March for Our Lives • 202
Cone • 204

The Crossing

after crossing the border
our village kin anointed

with blood, the earth behind
us kissed a last time, with

fingers on brown hands
pointing north like the surest

way to Eden, the quiet birds
in curious stare, in a darkened

universe that makes us tremble
before coming light, our ears

are tuned to lying words like
arrows in wait. we crawl the

final distance into the North
the bodies of those who did

not make it still cooling in
the desert night in shallow

graves, our tears swallowed
up by the curved darkness

of a strange new world, the
piteous wails of children in

tow with scraped knees, and
the fatigue felt from dragging

lingering fears. once we are on
the other side, we will pray

for God to make small the
loathing tongues and violent

acts that leave us without a
drop of life and distant yet

from Eden.

Shithole

these are not pious times
with politicians reflecting
in the company of grace, or
a president detached from
the sinful impulses of hate.
the dispatches report daily
the lunacy of Trump who
with his faithful band tramples
on the weak, Black, Yellow,
Red and Brown. in this time of
sorrow Angels on Pennsylvania
Avenue pass the White House in
flight calling on memory, decency,
reason and faith to strip the perfect
emptiness from the man who panders
to White Supremacists and reduces
whole nations to the vulgar slang of
his intolerant tongue. in these times
loathing keeps its shape, spreads it
messages by the seconds, pounces
on its victims, and unflinchingly says
this makes the nation great! these are
not pious times, so let us begin to carry
America in fractured pieces to her well
dug and brand named grave.

Color

do you remember that first
day the roosters crowed in

the next-door apartment to
step out of the dark, inhaling

the smell of peeled oranges on
the carts heading to Southern

Boulevard with old men, the
intoxicating odors of a season

that had us lean into the day not
thinking of the reeking streets. do

you remember climbing on top
of it to gallop past the procession

of church goers dressed up like
it mattered to heaven, the pigeons

taking flight from us, the invisible
rushing down the street with us past

the old Cathedral where nothing ever
happened. do you remember losing

yourself in the little things of the
block, smiling at grandmothers with

shopping carts, the lost look on the
pale faces of Roman collared priests

trying to figure out how to name the
things they really love. dear brother,

I adore the way yesterday hands me the
splendor of such things, how that time

never yelled at us for speaking Spanish,
or having sweet brown skin. I have the

pleasure of such days with you inside
of me, which lets me laugh in a world

too often dressed for mourning.

Rudy

I learned to walk the streets
carrying pieces of the moon
in my pocket to light the dark,
lumbering along the avenue
thinking about the Lord without
a single piece of the promised land
priests talked about in mass and
grandmothers whispered was closer
than my brother. I passed the troubled
church bells not far from the lily shops
on Jerome Avenue and the windy spot
where you dear brother lifted your eyes
to the Cathedral that forgot your
name long before you sighed a last
good-bye. I learned to walk along
disbelieving good news, aware the
filthy streets were closer to me than
the sweetly silent Lord. I walked the
very block where you were delivered
to the arms of death, stood quietly on
your exit stain beneath the stars, and
said your name however foolish the
sound for the ears of the One who too
expired before his time at your very
age in a place called Golgotha.

Lost Name

you have been here long
enough to lose your name,
wonder about the looks of
of the world escaped, the
last dirt road walked in the
shoes you wore across the
border, and the long night
of saying farewell. you have
been here long enough to say
the fortune-tellers at the little
church know too little about
your world of laments, the
loss of a mother to a soldier's
gun, your sister skinned by
his bayonet, and his death
dealing shots responsible for
making orphans with dirty
cartridges that everyone knew
were American made. you have
been here long enough to hear
the whispered words of those
recounting measureless pain,
the terrifying images of Jesus'
followers hanging from trees,
and to complain to God who
circles the stars with justice
never seen. you have been here
long enough to demand an end
to the evil done by the crooked
money-grubbing bunch so far
from God—the witnesses who
weep with you know!

The Apartment

for many years she had lived
in the slum inside an apartment
wrapped in colorful cloth carried
from another country, receiving
friends on plastic covered living
room furniture into the deep night,
brushing the dust from the papered
roses carefully placed in pots in the
corners of her three rooms, never
giving a single thought to two jobs
held packing coats and cleaning
floors, unconcerned about the
feint light from the neighborhood
sky barely making its way into her
bedroom window, and kneeling before
an altar of religious relics to strain
after answers all day. for years she
had lived in that apartment waiting
for the mighty tears of God to pour
on the edges of her far-off world, to
flood sidewalks toward the promises
of this worldly glory, carry her in the
untainted currents of praise, and widen
her heavy heart with sweetly packed
mysteries. in her tiny paradise in the
old tenement that some would say is
unbearable, she listened for the wind
to fly strongly into her dark rooms to
turn her in sleep with good news from
the mountain top—I just love to sit with
her listening, too!

The Border

I crossed the border after
walking for miles with an
open mouth eating fresh
clean air and scraps of
corn and beans given to
me by old women who
promised to pray. alone,
at night, after staring for
awhile at a brilliant partial
moon, I pulled out the book
of lies to read a few lines to
see whether this time it would
convince me to believe in the
perfection on the other side of
the stars, in peace soon to come
this way like a blinking light at
a busy traffic corner that says
take the next turn to find the
promised land. I crossed the
border to discover a different
neverland, to live in a world
of stares that make God flinch,
work my farmers hands in city
days and stay out of sight each
long dark night. I left the place
where the air is brown, made it
to the choking English streets,
spend extra time in my large room
of memories, and look around for
loving kindness to hit me like a
glad verse from the book of psalms.

I crossed the border like Christ with
undocumented faith, a heart half-full
of doubt, and an old pocket Bible
deeply out of step. I crossed the
border to the land happy to march
strangers like me to the grave, while
yelling on the way there is no light
from heaven for wetbacks and spics!

The Scent

in the autumn of life age
delivers us to unsuspected

worlds where quietly we sit
to observe the leaves on the

fall trees gently touch earth.
we wonder about things left

undone, the pitch desires still
circling in our graying hearts,

the sweet bridges that brought
us far, the beauty that is much

deeper than changing form, flesh,
and bones. each day more loosely

laced, we feel the world young in
every part within, the memories

of reckless youth now giving us
sweet rest, and the things we love

alas not weak in each tasty living
breath. we live where time is no

longer complained, a place where
dreams sluggishly still make their

way into the light, the deeply hidden
spring that has held thousands of tears

and bathes us now with the scent of
heaven that was always near—this

we say delivers us!

The Storm

in our twenty-first century
the devastation of a storm
threatening to leave more
dead than anyone has the
strength to bury in soggy
ground exposes stars and
stripes sinking into a vast
sea. our flag placed on the
distant moon the hurt and
dying nightly see is like a
desert mirage for Spanish
speaking citizens who do not
count for the president as other
than spics! the sweet chariots
of God cannot even rescue the
condemned who live each day
afraid since the foul mouthed
head of a decaying democratic
State gives no crying damn for
flag or them!

The Sting

the history toward which
the country slides will be

memorized in the future
with indecorous words,

a bitter taste on tongues,
the sound of heaped up

wailing, and the Rose
Garden haunted by all

the anonymous dead in
the deserts, mountains,

cities, and islands in the
middle of vast seas. the

future made last week by
the president's tweets spread

ignorance across the land,
conceited tales ringed with

the scum of nothing good
done, and citizens swayed

by rabbit punching lies to
live quietly in these times.

the history the future will
bitterly speak, the stories

from the public squares, the
marches on town streets, the

abominable citizens who paraded
hate covered with white sheets,

the elected idiots who came to
their defense, will ask of every

resident whose precious life was
dressed with utter fright what

comes next?

The Garden

in my childhood on the
streets, I saw in the ripe
hour of each day things
spoken about truth in the
gloomy basement of the
church that were clearly
not true. I passed through
many sanctuaries, where
the good folks wasted dreams,
denied the long lines of sorrow
claiming their kids and waited
for the coming hour to lower
beloved innocence with heaps
of rotting flowers beneath the
earth. in loud hollow tones, I
heard voices by men trained to
think morally exhorting broken
hearts on the block to wait for
coming heaven and the aromatic
blossoming of the stony road. after
all these years, the wailing has not
stopped, the good news yet only
sweeps away the dust, priests are
glad in useless prayer, academics
have their cottage industry studying
our streets and Spanish eyes keep
searching for the promised land
confessing it's just too damn far
from here.

The Painter

woke up to hop the subway
downtown to get lost in an

art museum to look at oils
that imagined the unfinished

work of God, stroll the rooms
with creaky floors the grey world

doesn't visit, stare at the Picasso
using colors and lines to trick my

eyes, until a word jumped up to
say something about the beginning

of things. I wanted to find somebody
to tell of an old woman on the block

living on the ground floor of Lefty's
building who painted at night. She

must have had a special set of eyes
to see things in the dark, to have the

night come to her like water rushing
down a steep hill, then capture on a

canvas details thrown her way by
whispered ghostly streets. I looked

for the associate curator of the cubist
wing, while repeating a few lines in my

head about having him come down to
the barrio to have a look at the paintings

this Abuela boxed and placed in a room
with a window facing the Westchester

Avenue. I found him talking casually
about Goya, Picasso, Orozco, Caravaggio,

and Manet in a near empty room, a small
voice in me said what the hell you can't lose

anything inviting the curator to visit the
block to talk with an old painter woman

about art—so I did.

Devotion

the evening shades are creeping
away as you sing morning prayer

expecting some great Spirit to drift
nearby with greetings. you lean to

whisper in the wind something about
being put a long way from fear in the

unknown coming day that threatens
frail bodies with workplace raids that

never leave foreigners in peace. your
troubled dust has been up in the early

morning for months holding tightly to
the hope that Angels would shortly come

and slip you a pass to basically live, take
you away from the shackles of evil States,

and allow your thoughts to breathe. you
will continue these morning prayers until

the long road you have taken North gives
you rest, the Bethlehem star is once again

in sight, and the world that hates your
company confesses the presence of a

divine-king in your brown Spanish
speaking face!

The Substitute

the school bell rings to call
pupils inside for the start of
a fresh day of learning. in
class a substitute eagerly waits
for everyone to take their seats,
then announces they will spend
a little time reviewing newspaper
clips for current events. the teacher
graduated from a local city college,
the kind filled with the children of
immigrants who speak in tongues of
the good news that led their family
name to North American shores.
Mr. Laboda dreamed himself into
the teaching world, filled with the joy
of leaving a speck of himself in kids
who will learn to unveil the dark for
themselves, and keep imaginary sails
within them from slack. that morning
the students discussed New York Times
headlines, the errors of government, the
misunderstandings burning houses down,
the fear of foreigners, bombs dropped on
Afghan heads, the dried blood papers find
a thousand ways to ignore, and the tilted
telling of truth.

War Drums

I visited the well-lit corner
on the other side of Southern
Boulevard in that time of day
everyone kept telling me too
many kids forget a needle with
dope coped on the block would
leave them dead. after the mounting
years of war this country has used to
to count passing years, I particularly
recalled Viet Nam protesters gathered on
that very spot unpacking their Spanish
objections in the name of bringing home
the neighborhood poor who were dying in
jungles for rich men's greed, far from
diplomacy and the requirements of peace.
on that specific day, I saw Manolo's mother
standing on the spot pouring her life in
tears, since her son came from the jungle
just to die in a tenement hallway with a
needle fixed in his veins. she whispered
into my ear, whenever the country is at war
the poor kids around here stop dreaming of
big things, and Tío Sam carts them away to
become citizens that die in the ghastly lands,
and for what! I carry this corner with me each
day praying for the war drums to stop their tenacious
beating, always asking the good Lord to soften the
the stone hearts of the men responsible for sending
poor kids to die in the name of their arrogance and
gluttony.

Waiting

I was born in the arms of
a tender world with voices
beneath a greying city sky
telling stories of penniless days.
slowly I began to crawl guided
by small lights on the block, to
walk in its varied dark, and grow
older in a wreckage field of Spanish
names. I watched buildings go
up in flames in the arson days of
those who never felt this land a
welcome place. I listened in many
tongues to the conceited excuses
explaining why in the barrio people
are undone, our hopes steered into
ignominious graves and our lives
treated like filthy specks of dust.
someday, when night approaches the
morning light, the blind start to see,
and the world moves a little closer to
truth, our hellish gates will unlock
and the wailing in this forsaken land
will come to a just end.

Bricks

one long summer morning, I spent
the time trying to count the bricks

that lifted the tenement six stories
high. the wind laughed when it blew

by the stoop where I sat in the rather
hopeless eye-opening task that made

people on the way to work slowdown
to stare at me like a miracle was on its

way. I restarted the count more than
once, pausing until the restless sidewalks

held still and the singing coming from
the storefront church filled with brown

feet for an old-fashioned time of praise,
stopped. my thoughts wandered about

that day making me feel like an actor in
a Tennessee Williams play forgetting

lines. without yielding a single inch,
I kept counting those bricks expecting

an accurate reading would deliver me
to the mystical heaven so many talked

about on the block. then, tired I stopped
counting and promised to try some other

time without stumbling on cracks and
shades.

The Shore

in the thanksgiving month of
November beyond the high

thoughts perjuring history
that make you gasp for air,

kind hands reach for you from
the aching depths known too well

by strangers in this land troubled
by mouths full of loathing. despite

generations of knowing the nation's
rivers, mountains, oceans, forests,

valleys and lakes, you are a stranger
here, one of the many dispossessed

of a place to call home, and your sweet
dreams are curved by those in power to

satisfy their English only wants. in the
many months to come you promised to

put away these days by having your truth
carried by the wind to any public stage,

where with elegant rage it will speak
to say America is home!

Resurrection

in this light, you do not walk
alone the long stony road, the
blessings of the heavenly stars
keep pace with the simplest joys
that meet you and your unbearable
tears. in this light, the church bells
are loudly ringing with good news
for a dirty world in need, with prophecies
remembered, and life without harm. in
this light, call out in the dark the saintly
names, whisper to the unifying mystery
that with firm clarity you know where to
stand. with your clay feet, dance the entire
length of life until you dive into the loving
arms of God.

Spanish Harlem

I roamed around the city by
riding her trains to places ten

year old eyes had never seen
way over on the side of town

that never heard of dividing
tracks. I roamed for years the

streets of Spanish Harlem in the
moonlight, looking for vanished

friends, traces of a dead brother,
collecting the storied dreams of

dark kids who ran, played and lived
in Spanglish where their world entirely

began. after years of climbing over
shady streets, I learned to stand quietly

on the corner to watch the dreams that
followed kids to school, grandmothers

into church and old men to tattered seats
carefully placed in front of Joey's grocery

store. I learned the words in school books
carried around the city never coughed answers

for spics. tell me, how long until we cross
the river Jordan?

Ivory Tower

in the tower made of books
surrounded by planted trees,
beautiful flowers, and seeded
grass, separated from barbarous
clashing on the streets, scholars
are busy measuring what God
says on pages kept on shelves
away from the poverty giving misery
a home on earth. here on this corner
where indifference habitually makes
its bed frail dark bodies crying from
afar are rarely asked to give witness.
on the streets where hands are joined
by the poor dressed with bells like lepers,
there will be no rest until the bitter wells
are sealed tight and the high-minded blather
is thrown into fiery depths!

The Protest

I knew the time would
come to take up the poor's

quarrel at City Hall, talk with
vigils to elected officials about

the bare bones economy scarcely
putting roofs over our heads and

dread on kitchen plates. I knew
the time would come to fling harsh

Spanglish words in the bright light
of day till Angels came looking brown

like us with beautifully spread
wings to make the deaf politicians

walk down the municipal steps
to listen. I knew the time would

come to lean on the shut doors
locked with the bullshit spinners

inside of them and open them wide
enough to break their hinges—that

time is now!

Factory Work

the toy factory where
his mother went to work

was then the only place
hiring broken English

girls with sleepy brown
eyes and dark faces born

on someone else's land.
she assembled toys with

smiles peeking each day
through her lips, and making

defamatory gestures behind
the white foreman's back who

had thick disorderly hands. one
afternoon the girls drenched in

tears who had the good sense to
join a labor union went on strike

to fight like gods to win their living
wages and safer times on the assembly

lines. they even said the strike was
the kind of prayer Jesus heard loud

and clear enough to make him take a
stand against the dreaded boss's fingers

that rested too often on their Puerto
Rican hips. for years she worked in

the toy factory listening each day to her
broken English making sweet sounds like

the grandmothers who came to America
young to give children their best made

dreams. one day without prior notice,
the mother realized these kids feed oatmeal

before school were living a history better
than her years spent wrinkling in a South

Bronx factory.

The Raid

this morning last night's
workplace raid is over, the

waiters are busy sweeping
sidewalks in the dim light

of a broken moon, a new day
starts them thinking about

rounded up friends in federal
cages who for thousands of

miles will sing the beauties
they are denied and the foul

ignorance bruising them once
again. frightened, the locked

up call out, bitter tears dropping
to the jail cell floor from their

brown cheeks, their lungs inhaling
the stale air that discloses the hate

chiseling grave stones in the dark
with Spanish names. the customers

start arriving for a first meal and
the waiters left behind wonder how

long the country will feed on lies
carefully wrapped like bible story

gifts!

The Spot

I sat behind the little park tree
like it was in the rain forest in
the ascending light of a chilly
morning. the Fort Apache police
parked their car next to the bloody
stain at the other end of the patchy
grassed park, where a young mother
moaned, a priest prayed and the
kids on the block who passed the spot
on foot each day claimed they saw
an Angel with long hair looking over
it. I waited quietly for the beauty of
the block to come walking down the
street, speaking loudly about glorious
things to come, pointing to the paths
calling us to walk with enormous strides
to the very end of the road where neighborhood
church bells ring. whenever tired of the
misaligned world, I would go to that spot
calling on South Bronx spirits to make
dark voices still. I often laughed with
the browning leaves blown by the wind
in that little park that was hidden from
the rest of the city and was comforted by
its sickly trees and song birds kept just
right for my barrio streets.

Latino Heritage Month

at the border, the guards
have already forgotten this

month belongs to the broken
who are walking to the barrios

to anglicize a new generation
of names, survive its gangster

violence, make homes far from
odious gatekeepers, and dream

with their new American children
beneath the Northern stars. on these

shores, the men who run the government
long ago proclaimed this month a time to

praise the Spanish speaking faces of America,
but social facts arrest such history by telling

a different story of the Browning of the nation
that keeps making us suspects and foreigners

on this land. someday, the country that fought
a civil war with the help of some ten thousand

Latino bodies for freedom will fall to its knees
to chant we shall overcome with us.

Prayer

a few pictures
stored in a shoe
box, an image
of a cinder block
house with a ribbed
tin roof on an old
dirty street, a still
life painting on a
wall brushed when
life was younger, a
tapestry hanging in
a cramped kitchen with
delicate blues, browns
and reds hinting a last
supper. the clamoring
of an unsettled heart, the
cursing shadows that
never rest, and evening
prayer answered by love
songs from above reaching
across the sweet ineffable
stillness.

Look Here

what do brown hands say
about sweeping floors, emptying

trash, tending yards, building other
people's homes, taking care of the

privileged kids, fear of the next raid,
the history of exclusion based on the

color of skin, writing on the walls of
homeland security detention cells,

and the American born children they
may not see for years? what does the

undocumented human being have to
say about children in public school,

covered in grass on the soccer fields,
growing up citizens in a hateful world,

strolling the sidewalks in an iron cage,
waking nights consumed by fear, and

listening to the news shows that say
anyone with a Spanish name is a god

damn alien here? when will politicians
talk about the taxes brown people without

papers pay, their daily hard work to make
a nation great, the days on the hill ignoring

their crucified lives and the coming future
with lots of colored skin? when will they

learn the names of the undocumented and
deportees, the fault of foreign policy for

poverty and graves, and the reason for
underground tracks these days? tell me

what day of the week will this so-called
Christian nation declare brown people are

human beings? when will the American
church bells ring for Spanish dreams?

The Decay

the enchanted island
in the Caribbean Sea,
its chain of mountains,
dense rain forest trees,
tucked away caves, deep
blue waters, cascades, rivers,
snaking rivers, dancing brown
bodies, sofrito dreams, African,
Indian and Spanish in me, is the
place the hellish rich man with a
fat belly full of lies and loathsome
views for the black and brown skinned
refuses in this sacred world to see. after
the storm, truth will heave a load of
shit his way.

Imagine

imagine life with a religion
only practicing kindness, the
streets for a church, the East
River pure, the mountain lakes,
and waters of the sea providing
gracious benediction. imagine life
the great teacher delivering truth
along with a few smiles and planting
wisdom inside you. imagine love in
every color of skin, a cool evening gale,
a forest of thick trees, nature breathing
free and blissful stillness in all things.
imagine religion true, the world with
perfect harmony and life separated on
earth from want, suffering, war, tyrannies,
and hate. imagine religion delivering to
us mercy, justice and sweet grace—at last
no flesh would rage!

American Dream

we have been living on the
block for several generations,
reaching back to the days
smoke blew from stacks that
lined the rooftops, the time
when Boricuas found jobs
with busy schedules in plants
alongside Jewish, Italian and
Irish friends. we walked the
streets together talking in tongues,
grins inspired by sweet broken English,
even crying by the arm about a world
distant from the American dream. we sat
for hours on stoops staring up at the
stars, imagining somewhere in that
deep space our different names were
beautifully known, talking about the
walks taken by others who quick stepped
here from the Southern border, and
then turning our attention to the way
the years chased us to the places on
the block struggling to rise from the
dust. How long can we last? America
will you ever see your face in us?

Faith

give me the faith
of simple kind eyes
where hope will never
hide, the faith of early
Spring evenings with
children running freely
on the streets, the one
wintry darkness will
never dare come near,
the kind in human wrong
made flesh to leave us
in the arms of love, the faith
that sweetly begs to smile
plodding lonely nights on
the streets. give me a faith
that sings the missing notes,
lifts laurels of peace in a world
of need, helps us see the mystery
that comes with thundering wind
to scatter words from scripture
with utter charm. give me a faith
that does not scream, never says
life is nothing but dust and will
not in the face of divine silence fade.

Rise

for months, we have waited
reviewing news reports daily
to announce decisions about
broken homes mended, empty
stomachs filled, the poor with
living wages, strangers from
other shores carried by Angels
down the streets, the God who
holds gay hands with love, the
hope of battered women on the
city curbs who shriek, and the dark
carpenter in front of hoisted flags
who without reluctance drops to
a knee. for months, we have
scanned the press that reports sad
stories of the malignant imbecile
who practices the finest obscenities
of speech on the innocent, decrepit,
vulnerable, different, excluded, and
weak. for months, we have waited
for love to cast a spell in hardened
hearts, to keep them from the fake
president's lies, to beat justice on
the White House steps, and say
the trampled condemned to death
will rise!

The Talk

we sat in silence for a long time
the morning you said you had a

father once who slipped away at
night through cracks in the living

room wall. you talked of injuries
collected by the dozens after he

left, jars full of tears in your tiny
bedroom, and nights of trembling

beneath your bed recalling the way
he thundered in the other room. I was

that day a quiet witness searching
for a way to meet you at the edge

of light, cleaning moldy words
inside of me for something to say

about the joy felt for your birth into
this world that should have long ago

drowned in your tears. you spent
all these years collecting and selling

the bright colors of the South Bronx
sunset, the joyful sounds of the local

church, the songs of brown children
running down the streets, and bagged

miracles for the people who cry God
take pity on me. again, we sat together

after all these years, like nothing had
ever been said confessing with retiring

smiles days were never simple.

Fifth Avenue

walking up fifth avenue
following prayer in the

Cathedral, tearful knowledge
escorting each step, while you

watch the hot dog vender on
the Rockefeller corner smile

at a man with a cigarette pressed
between his lips placing an order

surrounded by smoke. you think
about the God you never saw

on the rooftop with little kids
propped against the skyline doors

damned to death by dope filled
needles nailed in their arms. on

the long walk to the block you
fumble around with the idea of

life giving bread said by the priest
to have risen from the dead for the

nameless living in the cursed apartments
of the South Bronx. your head shakes in

the shadows keeping you company the
closer you come to the restless doors of

apartments on the block, where hard working
people loudly cry out at night complaining of

never seeing heavenly signs that matter. you
tell yourself, the day this bitterness is tasted

in the Cathedral, praying will march and the
sacred bread will be sweet to the taste.

Daily Bread

this daily bread wiping
away the tears pooling in

exhausted eyes, shared on
day laborer lines formed

each morning at the 7/11,
tossed around work sites

where divinity with us is
exploited and crushed by

the stiff passing of time
carrying our dreams on

its back, sometimes gives
us peace. we wake up each

morning to say prayers and
weep to convince divinity

somewhere to speak to a world
so inhospitable to its brown

undocumented kin. this daily
bread inside of us, finds us in

despair and allows us today
the impenitent wish to shove

the cold hearted far, and father
still away.

American Shore

I speak to you now of
the dozens of ways those

who walked for miles
feel defeated by revolting

words that come at all
hours, prance around in

public and make them spill
any sense of hope. yet, in spite

of all the things they suffer in
the long history curving on

the English named streets, the
memories soaked with the muddied

waters of the river called their
Jordan, the gatekeepers who

call human beings like them
illegal, the rules telling citizens

to name them criminals, the
countless nights of trembling

at the altar rail and in detention
cells, these precious least of God

will continue to come like the
waves of the vast sea that beat

against the American shore.

Stony the Road

in our sorely wounded days
walking grubby streets, we

wait for you to speak in the thin
faces of strangers, long to see

you hiding in the yellowing eyes
of neighborhood drunks, and find

you taking refuge in the Puerto
Rican girls' hopscotch game. Lord,

we have asked you questions on
the saddest days, heard the men of

currency speak of us with filthy
words, and listened for you to tell

us when to expect delivery from this
world. for the sake of the holy water

we still collect at church, the pure
sounds of the sacred voices that sing,

the blessed metal clanging from the big
steeple bells, the crosses dangling on

our necks, are you really keeping watch
over us? Lord, tell us are you the all-seeing

being coming to us in dreams, then save
us from the exhaustion of the wilderness

each step we take in America with purest
darkness does trace. Lord, tell us will you

give us life in this here and now before
calling us to slumber beneath brown earth?

we promise to listen to what your words
watered by our daily tears have to say.

Ancient Shore

the junkie living up the
street in the abandoned

building empty for two
years, fell down the steps

on his way to mass in the
basement of the church, the

one spot on the block beyond
apartment walls, where God

was always speaking Spanish.
after shooting up that morning,

he went to the apostolic place
on a whim, the voices of dead

friends in his head stampeding
the only places left to deny the

hell flowing in his veins, and
telling him not every priest on

the block is exercising crackpot
religion for a buck. he darkened

a pew behind candles dancing in
front of the image of a brown Holy

Mother, the smell of fresh cut flowers
filled him and widened his eyes to see

the blue-green mantle with scattered stars
adorning *La Morenita*, while her tender eyes

that knew him in the dark made life
more precious. he exited the mass on

his knees promising to deliver his
broken frame to the ancient shores

the Holy Mother walks with colored
people just like him.

Good Night

the simple day is
rounding the corner
sliding into last light
on its way to rest. I
see mothers with lullaby
lips holding children by
the hand singing on the
way home entirely with love,
not one insult can be heard,
not a whisper against the
nightfall, just infinite hope
like wings spreading over
the tired street. the evening
unfolds with chants about
precious dreams that spend
their days swinging in brown
hearts, wisely sharing stories
that make lids heavy, and still
causing something in us to wait
for the soft words that will whisper
in an ear before the placement of a
gentle kiss. when the morning light
makes its way to our side of the world,
we will be looking at the sky asking
God to come down.

Paradise

from these streets we have
sometimes seen our country,

caught a glimpse of the lights
shining downtown that leave

us in darkness, imagined countless
explanations to describe to children

their place on the block that is always
untouched by citizens who are never

in these parts speaking to them in
Spanish. we have spent many nights

longing for grace, gathering in the tiny
park to play congas to the sounds of

poetry spilling rapid fire from Spanglish
tongues, reading dark brown eyes in

bodies resting on the stoops wisely
disclosing neighborhood mistrust of

the politicians who promise they do
stand for us, but instead often unhinged

by the stories of bigotry enacted by
pale faces deaf to us. with crippled

beauty, we survive the singing-winds
of hate, and in our piece of the world

know and wait for light to leak into
the dark!

The Maid

when I woke up this morning
my mother who lost a factory job
was rushing out the door with
a bowed head on her way to
become a white family maid,
in a Central Park duplex in a
building playing pale American
music in mirrored elevators, smartly
dressed like a telephone book page with
slick writing. she kissed us adiós with
a look in her eyes that left three children
at the table speechless, but agreeing
to wear the kiss all day on their skinny
faces. after a long week of scrubbing,
washing, dusting, cooking, serving, bowing
and taking care of other kids, the money was
no less sickly green, and she appeared to age
a few years in her skin—we thought maybe
we can pray a little harder with our under
nourished tongues or eat a little less to help
out!

The Stranger

where stranger have you been
welcomed on earth like God
in need? the houses built on
sand over here reject the holy
presence you bring from a far
away land, the bitter bread and
wake of tears you carry through
the indifference of the world not
seen by many like the shouldered
cross it is. how often stranger have
you knocked on these American doors
to share stories of waking each morning
to the alarming hate that says the Word
did not become flesh? I think about your
dreams inside the gates, the penetrating
words on your trembling lips, those scarred
hands that spin the gold others keep, the news
to everyone and everything reported without
mention of your name, and this country obsessed
with the legality of being. stranger, those who
only have time for hate will one day be surprised
to know an undocumented God keeps you safe
and from the wretched grave.

Missed

our absent fathers left us
stories often talked late at

night of creatures unrestricted
by the dark, times of village

sadness and the dirt roads
so richly black walked by the

enchantresses with covered
faces and frightening glares.

they handed us a tradition
suited for the Bronx, tales to

keep us from the streets and
make us hungry for the other

world to which many of them
returned. one by one, they fled

angry bosses feeding on their
blood, the haunted city streets

tormenting their dreams, and
our hungry faces, illnesses and

grins. now, we talk until the
morning sun of meeting them

once again in flesh, bone and blood
joy leaping from our childish eyes

to say with a simple look your
migrant dreams never left.

The Room

the hotel room I rented
was big and new, nothing
like the one with the torn
sofa, where we ate our bread
talking about all the feet on
the old splintered floor. I can
still see the photo hanging
on a bare wall of Rudy with the
goatee sketched by me to make
his six-year-old face a little more
deep. sometimes, I see the old
room just looking out the window,
on mountain tops with villages in
fog, in the soothing blue waters
of Tulum my ancestors swam for
years, in the cracks in a single leaf
tumbling to the earth, and those
spots within searching for home.
why am I telling you this, it's just
a room from my precious slum, a
place where family long gone sat
with friends to talk knowledge of
a better world, a space that still
hangs around in me.

The Reach

darkness has descended on
those looking up at the flags

streaming in the wind before
the house that has given little

to any. truth is an irregular
show from the man who speaks

only English and plans ruin for
foreign speaking tongues with

reckless cruelty, poison words
and an uncanny skill for hate.

at his Rose garden parties, doubt
never seeps into his tongue, standards

of decency are always absent, and
the city winds lament carrying his

foul smelling tongue. now, it seems
each day starts dim, and we squawk

like crows in abandoned school yards
of democracy near gone. darkness has

descended on the nation's streets, but I
assure you the most exquisite hearts know

history will deliver the last word of truth
about the con man in the White House

and his racists sack of lies!

Morning Light

when the sun from the east
begins to rise to stir morning
from sleep, everything once again

takes us to places shaped carefully
in last night's litany of surprises.
we look up at the fading stars behind

moving clouds that seem held by a single
thread and see the things that fly in the air
collecting pieces to turn night into day.

they swoop beneath the bridge at the end
of the lane pushing through what is left of
the evening and with each dive toward the

waking earth ask with air knocking wings
did you dream! the same old chair invites
us to sit and ponder a little about what is left

of the hush dark, and we silently imagine
rumors of peace and church bells that
ring loud to show us the way to ancient

Palestine. the new day rises with enduring
love, paradise on earth walking in the flesh,
melodiously chanting of mystical delights in

the valleys, the hills, the rivers winding out to
sea, and the city streets. and we, finally are
content to hear the voices beneath a ripening

sky cry out—Good day!

Mi Barrio

I felt the barrio in my veins
like a tired river with no place
to take shade, like bones never
to rise at the sound of Ezekiel's
wrenching cries, like broken hands
no longer to feel a day of work,
and suspended in a wicked junkie
trance. I felt thirst left in my throat
by the empty cup handed to me by
the block priest, thought about the
precious words uttered by his lips
to terrified people on Bronx streets,
wondered what the keeper of the
church would say about the bundle
of flowers tossed in the ground for
the kid with a dead tongue that will
never speak, again. I pushed
a tiny candle into the crack of the
neighborhood Cathedral wall, struck
a match to make it dance a flame and
cursed the pious tradition seeping
through the partition with a narrow
vision of life for us. I felt dope pouring
in my veins yelling the whole way, the
day will come for the trampled,
the day will come when Christ will no longer
cover the same wounded distance without
uttering a single fucken word!

The North Side

on the boulevard stretching
all the way to the rich white
neighborhood on the northern

side of town there are markets
packed with all kinds of food
the hungry cannot buy with

moneyless pockets. the little kid
with the jacket with the words
South Bronx pressed on its back

stands in front of the A&P the
whole day long waiting to help
one of the old ladies from the

block carry groceries home for
a tip. he saves every coin in the
front pocket of a pair of thrift

store jeans, then buys a big ole
bag of fries to cook for his two
sisters, before heading up to the

roof to complain to circulation
clerks in heaven about the state of
affairs on earth for the poor. in sickness,

hunger and thirst, he never kneels
to spell out his case to the sandal
footed man who has seen earthly

light, and knows too well the empty
nights and graceless fate of those who
live with unanswered prayer. I wonder

how long until the good Word does
something sacred like filling these
empty stomachs? How long until

it wipes the tears away from our barrio
eyes? How long till the meek collect
their earth?

Sutherland

this year death has torn
open our hearts from public
squares, to schools, movie houses,
parks, malls, and the sacred halls
of church. in the circles made
for prayer, no one even imagined
more than twenty-four thousand
innocents dropped by the barrel of
guns into the earth's dark void. when the
glad times are recounted, we will remember
to speak of the black cloths laid on the boxes
of the dead, holding hands for yet another evening
prayer, and the everlasting despair making us in so
many different ways ask of you God what have
the victims done to make you so weak for them?
before the year ends, we will sing and pray in the
midst of darkness to proclaim you are still light,
but say you really hear the howling, deeply feel
the hurt, and clearly see the bitter tears? Oh, dear
Emanuel, break your centuries old silence and tell
us who to blame!

Weep

weep for the children
shot in schools, the parents
who now grieve, the siblings
filled with gloom, friends left
with broken hearts, the country
allowing it to happen, yet again.
pour out a sea of tears for the
politicians of the NRA, for sunken
faces beside the graves, the gods
who spin the world in the dark,
and those now dead before their
time. drop down to your knees
to listen to the trembling lips in
prayer, the red tongues shouting
the souls despair to the turning
clouds in heaven. weep with me
for the children bullets claimed,
let them not be still, but make you
listen, then hurry to protest the
senseless loaded guns.

Enough Practice

I have lived through a century
of a world at war, listened to
news of it unending, wept for
the nameless whose light was
senselessly darkened, waited for
the words thou shalt not kill to
march in our hearts, and few are
there to give peace with justice
a chance. I have listened to the
voices in the wilderness, the ones
shouting ahead of the bloodshed,
the gunshot wounds, the bombing
raids, the quarrels of religions that
end in death, the thirst of humanity
for the damp grave, and the call away
from evil in our hearts, then asked
myself what next? I have prayed
for the death of hate, and the gentle
lighting of love to slowly become
without harm reality.

The Meditation

the patient night offers
a gentle breeze for silent
sitting, the soft drizzling
of rain leans south to reach
the brown cheeks of strangers
who have come a long way
stepping too quietly for anyone
to hear. the night continues to
march around us, the birds in
silent watch can see sadness
leave without smiles after each
deeply drawn breath. you start
whispering to Angels and the
mild spirits of the earth in all
the ways you learned on the
other side of the border, and I
sit quietly beside you washed
clean by your indomitable faith.
when the clouds clear, we gaze
at the stars together imagining the
great mystery that pours mercy
on the fields, the rivers, mountains
and deserts, the One that moans
with us on earth, and arrives on
time for love.

Homeless

I remember sitting on a park
bench in Greenwich village

the yellow cabs driving by
filled with English chatter,

people who walked making
long speeches, the smell of

flowers placed at one end of
the park, where the pavement

leads to couples seated closely
to tempt love. I remember the

old accented men playing chess
with looks in their eyes expected

of those who measure the weight
of air, the small crowds that gathered

around them, the twitter of birds new
to the city, the lights coming on in fancy

building windows as if they were jealous
of the dark, and with half closed eyes

laughing with strangers. I remember
the drunks who stumbled in each other's

arms, were ignored like useless dust,
relieved themselves behind trees, and

shouted out their names. but I remember
under the stars imagining Angels chasing

me around the park, over benches, up a
few trees, past the bikes chained to no

parking signs, until exhaustion set in to
ask what business do you have for us?

The Kitchen

the kitchen talk came with
tossing corn with beans for

a whole day to aid children
thousands of miles away. the

women smiled in the spaces
between words lost in stories

about the long walk north with
no map, knowledge of where to

find the north star and stumble
after stumble in the dark. they

remembered sleepless nights on
the walk, waiting in the cold,

standing in ditches, bristling at
the sight of headlights, and from

their limitless hearts turning to
the images of sons and daughters

though far away cheering them
on. they laughed while stirring

a pot of black beans, then suddenly
broke into whispers about cooking

food to earn a few coins for children
with nothing of their own to have a

bit more light in their eyes. they were
silent for several minutes then like risen

from the dead, they agreed a long day
in the kitchen for a cause to bid farewell

to the fear and sadness resting in their
hearts was worth it—hallelujah they

shouted as heads turned!

Nevertheless

it was dark into the new morning,
the splintered wood floors in the

abandoned tenement creaked with
the weight of big city rats stepping in

cold rooms, but Jesus with his crown
of thorns and holes in his hands was

not among the guests. the man was absorbed
in thought about the holy indifference

that never says a word about the clenched
teeth streets, the intravenous breakfast

taken by kids, and the restless poor that
beg to be saved. his mind was poking

about distant memories of the lanes on
a mountain side that led to playing fields

with kids chasing foot balls while colorful
jubilant birds watched, the smell of peeled

mango in the air, mothers huddled on the
grass giggling about intimate secrets, and

siblings in hugs. he wondered whether or
not the celestial grammar of renewal had

learned anything from the suffering down
here?

Hit

I noticed walking down
the street lately no music

booming from the upper
story windows, the buses

no longer making the wind
sing, and the rising sun

seldom coming around the
block to embrace us. why?

the excited voices on the
boulevard that yelled holy

mother of God to wipe the
dust from hundreds of hearts

were quieter than ever, while
dark colored jeeps roamed

along the street with people
who can't speak Spanish in

them carrying handcuffs on
belts, pistols on their hips, and

shoes for a swift run. why? I
stopped to talk to the piragua lady,

a citizen of the United States, who
stands on the corner selling coconut

ice cream with pinches of smuggled
hope for strangers, afraid. I thought

with her about how to tell the little
kids to dream like beautiful brown

migrants whose lips say there is
good to come, a place sickness on

earth forgets, a world where kindness
waits for them in pitch black dark!

The Dark

in dark times the eyes begin
to see, the murmuring hearts
whisper about the rough edges
to clip, and from the bedroom
windows in these buildings the
streetlights over the sidewalk
appear specked by moths. the
harsh times are afraid tonight
to stir beneath a moon offering
aid of light, you blink to clear
memories worth forgetting like
dust, then shout at the shadows
the wrong names of God to see
who will dare show up.

Old Streets

this morning tapped me on the
shoulder with a gentle light
floating in the sky. I walked
around the neighborhood to
see what it had to offer passing
buildings that told the stories of
past generations that spoke in
different tongues, feeling cold
air press against me like it was
trying to open the curtains of
my half-deserted heart, watching
the streets get sprinkled with the
early morning risers whose voices
were slowly waking, pondering
beneath the ceiling of retreating
stars, after all, was the trip worth it
for those who came from afar, living
with the atmosphere of their kids
in grassy tombs, and labor to the
bone in a land that wounds them
each day? I walked past the block
windows imagining the mothers in
the apartments at that hour kneeling
in front of their altars, inheriting a
world of sacred love, pouring into
the widening day the kind of hope
that makes a life to speak of, and
decided to keep treading until I sent
confusion about these old streets to
the finest avenues, tenements and
dreams.

Innocence

Eden unseal your tightly
sealed gates, come to the
ruins where we walk, hold
us with your certain hope,
disclose your whereabouts
in the mountains, the rivers,
the deserts, the bushes, the
trees, the streets, the cells that
gather us to weep. Eden tell us
the garden is home for Maria,
Julio, Jesús, Tomás, Lupe and
Juan. when we open our eyes do
not ask us to leave, taste disobedience
on our lips, see our hungry years in
the flesh, stand with us on the city
graves to weep and tell God to end
our banishment. Eden become one
of the meek, walk with the paupered
of the earth, fill your eyes with black
and brown tears, then deliver us.

Passing

a flower was pushing up from
the crack on a rock beside the
old building preserving beauty
in front of the tenement's splintered
bricks. a woman sat quietly in front
of the stone going over her life, flipping
through the pages of a Spanish speaking
bible, asking how much love would
make it into the day. words in her
head manufactured long thoughts,
revealing in her wrinkled eyes the kind
of patience needed to believe shrinking
divinity would show up in a blackening
world. she longed to sit longer in the
silence, reciting short prayers for the
block, filling herself with the tiny grace
growing from the stone, receiving the
laughter of children in the distance who
hopped off to school, but she got up to
carry her weary bones to her cleaning job
downtown, passing the neighborhood big
church where the priest was asleep.

The Martyrs

when the bells began to
ring on the 16th day of the

Holy Soul's month, smoke
had long poured out of the

flashing guns held by men
with covered hearts who came

for the lives of six Jesuits and
two witnesses. thousands of

martyrs the civil war made
with American bullets fired

from smartly finished guns,
in villages, fields, rivers and

hills where the black birds shrieked
over their blood, and not a single

tear was shed by soldiers for those
dropped. when judgement day arises,

we will bring the blood-stained clothing,
the bottled spattered brains, the screams

beyond the grave and the written names
of the authors of these crimes. on that

day, the stooges of death and forgetfulness
in the name of the innocent will be entirely

unmasked and their souls will burn with the
howling of our dead, then we will swing open

the doors to let out the certain things we have
seen that terrify our hearts and testify against

the official mouths for their years full of
silence!

Affection

there is much to be said about
the country left behind that spat
you out sending you to stalk about
these parts. in the days when
breathing a certain name was
a crime, and lighting candles to
draw truth near reason enough
to be tossed into Adam's grave,
you breathlessly took to the road
for miles hiding in wild foliage
across two countries, until you
reached the cover of the neatly
pruned English named trees. I
came beneath your spell listening
on the stoops, watching your slender
brown hands tremble whenever you
spelled out death in the places heaven
forgot to pity, hearing about the villages
surrounded by fields where the poor cried
out for the Sacred Mother, and seeing you
bent by tears recounting how many times
a day they call you worthless, illegal, and
criminal wetback filth. on the tar carpet
of the roof, I noticed one-night sitting
quietly beneath the stars, you tenderly
nursing a bruised lip God too felt, these
words you carved, "someday the land of
milk and honey will come." I looked at
you pleading with my eyes longing with
you for it to be quick.

Advent

we went to Mapes Avenue for
another look at the place the
building stood where Sonia
grew up, the sky pressing
grey clouds closer to earth,
memories packed away from
time to time rising with music,
the incarnate laughter of the
kids who ran up and down the
tenement steps sharply heard
in our heads, our eyes being
washed clean for the first time
in years by dim city light. the holy
teen child that lived in the building
had the habit of praying on the
roof holding a flashlight aimed
at the stars, then reaching into a
bag with bakery made bread she
insisted was a sacrament. Sonia
lived on this street unknown to people
piling up wealth on York Avenue, and
the politicians coming up with new ways to
enter into conflicts certain to deliver the
earth closer to the grave, but she made
a big difference to us. we stood there
a long time, hoping Sonia would again
leap onto the sidewalk with flowers in her
hair to talk to us about the best direction to
lob our deepest prayers.

Letter to the White House

I have long thought to write
this letter to the one in charge
for whom a new psychological
disease was named that makes
us throw up at the description
of its symptoms. I still find it
within the norms of reason to
send it to Pennsylvania Avenue
where, Mr. Trump, has become
the new tenant with a most cracked
view of the world to ever grace that
stately place. forgive me for not
presuming he has a speck of moral
decency hidden from sight that will
one day push its way to his regularly
exercised filthy tongue. excuse me while
I flip again the pages of Sinclair Lewis'
1935 novel of frightening times beloved
by nativists, remembering it didn't happen
here then, for FDR became president
freedom, equality, the working class
and the poor busily built democracy,
big business was restrained, streets,
roads, bridges, the environment given
a boost, civil rights were fought and
We, the people stood quite tall. But,
you first billionaire to be elected president
by Putin, a habitually failed businessman,
distressingly witless, harsh, and driven
by unimaginable rot have with your
authoritarian ways, eighty-two years

after the appearance of *It can't happen
Here*, give the world reason to fear. in
truth, you alone Trump are not to blame
for slipping out of the New York Tower,
help came from your Russian friends to
twist the standards of the presidential
election, indulge your vain ego, exploit
your imbecility, and push you on to victory
for the Kremlin's game. And, of course, tens
of thousands of citizens crazed by a politics
of hate and ignorance supported you in the
ballot box, their favorite illiterate reality TV
show thug. for now, allow me another
thought, presidents change in America,
and the contemptable leadership of the
fake president will be discussed in the
history books school boys and girls will
read with the gladdest heading to describe
him—Rubbish!

Love

on this darkening earth,
love is a faultless light,
a blessing on the corner
for simple holy flesh, with
gentle winds trembling
on our lips, in our souls
forever and mysteriously
fixed. from fickle heaven
it came to earth's savage
lairs, sweetly calling us to
her itinerant peace. I love
her kisses against my face,
the warmth of her flaming
embrace, her endless concession
of paradise and turning from
despair. when all is quiet on
the block, twilight brightened
by the stars, and God's long
years surprise us with speech,
I will confess no fitter thing
for me—this blameless light
can speak for the deaf, blind
and dead, the poor who walk
the streets, the migrants in the
flesh, the whole lot weighing
in for breath.

.

The Garden

we never set foot in
the garden or laid eyes on
the forbidden fruit it appears
from the witless vision
of the politicians many
have ingested. you see,
our unknowing souls have
for years wept about being
pushed by this country into
the dark, imprisoned by its
resonant blaspheming words,
in school, at work and within
our old tenement walls rendered
helpless by their calculated spells
designed to make us mourn the
dreams conjured on distant shores
beneath the sweetly moving sky. we
suspect someday our complaints will
sound loudly in heaven for the Maker
to carry out a new beginning with a lot
less, woe!

The Bus Ride

I set out from the city one
December day at dawn with
the winter moon bright over
the cold sidewalks, the bus

was being driven by an old
uniformed driver with a grey
captain's hat who greeted us
over a loudspeaker before

announcing the next stop and
final destination. I sat above
the front wheel bouncing for
hours, the odor of cigarettes

from the back of the bus making
its way to exit my slightly open
window. at one stop, I saw a young
woman trying to sell flowers, the

wind gently tossing her hair over
the bunched Roses held by her slender
fingers. I balanced my eyes trying
to see her clearly, my reflection in

the glass getting in the way, finally I
noticed her making change for a sale
like a magician performing a new trick
for a curious crowd. we picked up a

man in an old suit reeking of wine, reading
yesterday's newspaper, traveling he spoke
out loud to meet fate in the next big
town, where he likely planned to loiter

around the bus station and linger on
cots in the mission houses, until young
saddened Salvation Army workers gave
food and escorted him away. I reclined

the seat closing my eyes to let family
left on the block walk around in what
dreams came, thinking about the flower
I left on a useless chair for the ungodly

days that would surely visit the apartment
sheltering my young mother I then sorely
missed. the bus reached the Los Angeles
stop, where I snapped to attention and

despite loneliness with half-shut eyes,
imagined in my fourteen-year-old mind
rollicking with Angels wordy about salvation
soon to come for an abandoned Spanglish

speaking kid like me.

The Beach Day

Orchard Beach came alive
on weekend outings with the

sounds of Salsa playing along
the slightly over a mile beach

in the Bronx. people who came
on the number six train, carried

their feasts in bags to buses that
whisked them off to the water

that kept their names. in bare feet
and cut off shorts, I saw the Bronx

served with laughter, food, families,
and dance. I never heard the sound

of weeping on those beach days with
hard working people whose eyes were

opened to other things, listening to one
another till sunset, and imagining in their

hearts the island in the middle of the sea
closer than the puffing wind. I remember

breathing the centuries old air, observing
sea gulls drop light feathers, chasing

cotton ball clouds up and down the beach
with my brother, wishing to bag sand to

sell on the block, bottle the sounding and
praying for such days to never end.

Thanksgiving

I have a sentiment for this day
tipsy with thanksgiving. the Most
High leaping quietly from trees,
stretched across the sky, in touched
family and friends, and from the great
nothing breathed into being. perhaps,
the precious Word will sink into the
table bread, wrap around our hearts,
and loosen with herculean strength
for the world the mysteries of love.
perhaps, we can take these blessings
to hungry homes, children without
warmth, the hard-working poor and
the people God forgot. before this
day is done, I will step aside to pray
for the heavenly Host to keep the
promises so long ago made.

The Migrant

she traveled weeks across
several time zones listening
to languages making sounds
the tongues beating them out
alone understood. those who
earlier made their way waited
for her on the back streets of
the city, the dim buildings of
Spanish Harlem, and on the
sidewalks their halting footsteps
wandered. in her wretched flight
from poverty with weary clay feet,
she pushed on in the new country
with strange colored faces, harsh
stares, and avenues winos crowded
to plead for a handout and a little
bread to eat. she smiled at the bums
finding more rest than she had ever
dreamed, then pushed on to 110th
Street to find simplicity in rebirth.
she was met by a distant cousin
who still could not speak a word
of English, a little boy at her side,
schooled to skip between two tongues
and fulfill his mother's wishes, then
entering the old building for the first
time the migrant whispered to those
who welcomed her it begins. . ..

Faces

summer lasted forever for
the playful kids let out of

school in time to remember
their real names. they sat on the

stoops talking about nothing
of importance, while elders

moaned heading out to work
or talked with each other about

figuring out the magic recipe
to make them whole. the kids

sat on the building steps for
hours, the sun moving above

their heads like sluggish pigeons
wanting to be left alone, their fun

heard around the corner delivering
sweet rumors about lovely places

to rove. there was something very
special to their names, Angel, Jesús,

Mateo, Ana, Elizabet, and Miguel,
rigged from first breath for the land

of milk and honey, and so thoroughly
uncluttered by church. they turned

old on the block, spent years wrinkling
in raggedy apartments with little room,

breathing twisted hope still real
like the endless summers, recalled.

Politics

with our attention fixed on
politics, with so many elected
representatives who have not
read and think too little about
what they say, what is talked
about on the street is true, these
are not pious times. the insensate
politicians make us shudder with
their dreams, the man in the White
House full of curved speech, delivers
us to fear, laments and sobs—how
does this president and his colluding
legislators serve the interests of citizen
justice and peace? the coffee shops are
buzzing with the idea that brass-handled
coffins are being made in ten-hour shifts
with the Trump name to bury democratic
principles in a big old grave—these are not
pious times! what fire is still shut up in our
bones, what nobler strain of citizen is left,
who will roll around in the dirt to stop this
needless march to the garbage heap?

Simple

the music blared from a half
open window on a cold Autumn

day, simple things like bread and
light acquired precedence in its

plain sofrito sounds. outside streets
were populated with pigeons that

swooped down to the sidewalk
picking at seeds thrown from a

second story window, several
nuns floated pass in black and

white habits losing balance at
the curve, a little girl tried to

keep step with her mother, an
old Jewish man stepped out of

his building and walked toward
the storefront synagogue on the

South corner, the whistles from
the factories were blown in the

distance, bearing witness to the
places labor is sold, and the day

bowed to heaven without the aid
of a priest. little boys out on the

fire escapes were busy counting
buses, trucks and hot rod cars

and worries hardly mattered at this
end of the big old tired world.

Needle Park

I got off the subway
at 14th street to walk

uptown until reaching
the nights edge, along

the way occupied with
thoughts of trampled

things left behind by
heaven, the sight of

stray hanging tongue
dogs, shrieking winos

out of Midnight Express,
passed the hotels where

the global tribes sleep, the
street-walker corners beside

churches of disbelief, until
stopping on 103rd street for

a rest. on the needle park
bench, where trembling Angels

sometimes are seen by junkies,
I sat for a long time with wide

open eyes at thirteen trying to make
out truth in the dark. the needle

park bench has been loitering for
years in my head, nearly disclosing

the mysteries of common life, the two
languages I speak cannot name. I may

stagger from time to time now on these
long walks and my voice often whispers

in the dark, but I prefer to keep going
until reaching the place giving rise to

an unbearable need to kneel.

The Balm...

a new day fell into the world,
sweeping over the babbling streets,

measuring gestures on the block,
entering tired lives like a fog, and

bringing enchanted words to the long
nights in the blistered tenements, where

Spanish folk pray in a language too often
unrecognized by God. today, we dream of

sweet grass growing from the sidewalks,
the rich giving away their worldly things,

looking for what is not there, and pressing
our palms to the hand nearest heaven. with

a crooning wind, we dare now to shout
ancient truths like a night threatening

storms, to disturb city hall, jeweled priests,
and the pâté heads with our booming voices

up from poverty and wretchedness. today,
we are not your evil aliens, brown servants

with white chains, savage threats to liberty,
or objects of two-faced churchy love. today,

we are brown brothers and sisters the balm
of Gilead completes!

Things

the city kids
spend time
with curiosity
in worlds that
playfully
stare at them,
enduring age with
restless hope,
trying to make
sense of the subways
crying their way down
the tracks and the
schools making
their Spanish speaking
hearts descend into a
puzzling dark.
when you listen
to them talk,
you get an earful
of clumsy words
with humble light
pouring in,
sometimes
managing to
brilliantly land
in the very
places you're
blind.
late last night,
on the 1203 building stoop,
the kids were talking

about the color of skin
and wondering why
the church around
the corner, like the teachers
at school, were so
determined to scrub
them White—standing
in their company
I felt the sting.

Thin Walls

in the apartment next door mothers
obediently gather to offer a half-night

of prayer to a fading God they will
never stop nudging. I can hear the

sounds made by their mouths through
the thin walls, the occasional falling

of house keys, and their faith gently
laughing in the dark. I can't help closely

listening to their ringing tongues, imagining
how they find new ways to pull divinity down

to earth like a blouse tried on in a Southern
Boulevard bargain shop. the children who

have tagged along with some of the women,
are chanting their own songs in other rooms

of the prayer house pitched no doubt to the
gods of nonsense. the more I hear their urgent

tongues, something moves me to walk to the
window to survey the streets below for signs

of a little Eden, voices crying in the wilderness,
priests loitering on the stoops confessing their

sins, and the block Pentecostal preachers finally
listening. when these mothers next gather, I plan

to paste my ears to the wall in order to allow
their disquiet to deliver me to the place they

know and live.

The Library

that's it you came all this
way to masquerade in the
public library the role of a
clerk, you've crammed hope
behind the lending desk, and
forgotten the world left behind,
where you were a judge, till
dealers placed the scent of
death at your door step. the
truth aired about you in the
aisles with books of the same
country you fled, whisper
without eloquent expression,
to say nothing about you, while
wounding the saving Angel
that walked you this far. like
any other refugee, you have
learned to step in the shadows,
to slide into each day without
listening to the conceited nativists
whose darkness within withers the
beauty of colored life with their mouths
shouting, Get Out! their ghastly sounds
I've heard you say are no match for
the tiny drops of heaven that were
poured into your soul.

The Giver

across the street an old man
dressed in clothes found in

a bad dream box at St. John's
thrift shop makes birds from

balloons for kids. he speaks in
Spanglish sentences to them

something about climbing around
rooftops for a better look at things,

crawling in the tall grass down at
the creek where a few herons come

to fish, then clearing his throat the
chattering wrinkled face says for

you, Nena. on the stoop, Carmen
Julia, always thinking about her different

life, sits with her two young girls to say
the rosary, hoping the words drift for miles

across the city to the places where battered
people live. on this morning, the block

spreads her curtain to budge grace out of
a distant shell for the tired brown faces and

the old ones' swollen feet. the sweet Lord
will need to decide what to do, where to walk,

and how to untangle the world right here,
today.

Wordless

we have resigned to go into
darkness carrying only fragments
of what mattered most about what
the indigent carpenter who drew
to earth drops of grace spoke.
no matter how many times the old
hymns are sung, worldly reason
turns toward the raven winged
house on Pennsylvania Avenue
to give a nod to the man who has
found sundry ways to exile good
and turn prayer into a spectacle
of fifty lashes with a smile, then
away "losers" to the grave. I wonder
about the people pacing around the
church aisles, the good news in their
gated hearts that stumbles, the dice
the feeble politicians throw, and the
high-pitched cries aroused by the cold
hate that cannot bear light, mercy, justice
and love. from the look of things, Eden
must have only been a dream, and all
that good news talked up in churches
nothing more than a flickering flame on
a manicured altar the man with no fear
of God in his White flesh with rotten
breath blew away.

The Postman

el cartero
with a blue bag
dangling from
his left shoulder
delivered border
crossing letters
to the poor, bills
to the forgotten
and
welfare checks
to young
mothers who
gave showy
church people
reasons
to complain and
fill the
air with gossip.
in the thin
evening light
of the hardened Bronx,
the postman talked
at length with his boy
named Angel
about needles shooting
gloom into innocent veins
and
the kids on the block
wordless with bowed heads
nearing
the cheap wood money

buys for low-priced
graves.
el cartero had other
things to
say, but
instead
leaned back
in a tattered chair
to sit silently with
Angel watching
the night
sluggishly
peel, away.

Departed

taken from the passing seasons,
I can hear you arriving from the

catechism class driven to laughter
by the ignorant things an out of

touch priest tried with prayer to
put in your head. the creek where

you loved to swim till nightfall has
not changed much and the sapling

you grew beside now is stretching
her arms toward the sky appearing

to confess. I imagine it is your face
that piece of nature misses, the visits

you made on hot summer days for
disobedient dips, and the way you

warmly leaned against the young
darling. the raft you built from railroad

ties inspired by your reading of Huckleberry
Finn is gathering dust on the banks, waiting

it seems for your fresh brown hands like a first
lover to toss it in the river. no matter how long

ago you left this world, we stand from time to
time on the curving creek banks to call out

your name and correct the sadness left the
day you were taken from us.

Bridwell Library

light follows us up
and down the book

rows, the latest titles
lunging off the shelves

into the hands of those
wanting to move a bit

closer to heaven beyond
their bruises on earth.

we sit in the study carrels
late into night, aware of

our short journey, quietly
absorbing the history of

these magnificent Bridwell
halls, the words offered in

them precious like our need for
bread, the pages entered untouched

by specks of dust, the tiptoe rooms
we love that give us the best view

to see bewilderment on the run.
tell me what will the future offer

when this library is wired up the
hill? will we have reason to be glad

or weep? will the future make Bridwell
known or deliver her to senility and bones?

tell me when this other world comes
will it be a beginning or a chilling

run to the end?

The Gift

the box arrived today
prudently taped by abuelas'

hands, addressed in perfect
script in the four directions,

with a scribble of English on
one side in bold red letters saying

fragile. cautiously the thing
was opened like a book of secrets

in the barely furnished room, the
grinning faces of siblings on top,

old letters never mailed, a plastic
bag of medicinal herbs to drink,

a stick of sugarcane with a heart
drawn in black on it, a couple of

stones taken from village walks,
a prayer written out by a first grade

niece with a mother's instructions
to recite it whenever in need of

heartening mysteries, the north
disbelieves. the box was placed

in a corner of the room, where it
became a beautiful place to store

the deepest memories of a Spanish
speaking home, thoughts about the

Sunday mornings crammed with
grandmother's church and days

of sitting on the ground where the
mountain scratches heaven's back

to eat tortillas and beans.

Saint Christopher

he walked for hundreds of miles
across mountains, the desert sands,

and shallow waters caring a tiny
jar with the village priest's blessings,

a few ensnared Angels and the spirit
of Saint Christopher in it. placed in

his pocket the jar was invisible to
others who were making the same

vulnerable march hoping the border
would be turning dark with startling

fog to float them in. he moved each
day with orders from above without

a single chart, shouted into the nights
something about missing the arms of

those loved, and wondered about the
stories strutted in worship aisles and

North American streets that speak of
stoned faced men, women and even

kids hungering to drop people like
like him into the ground. his shaky

tongue and body made of wretchedly
rattling bones prayed for bitter eyes

to see a simple word of welcome
wipe away the endless tears and

make dead clocks turn toward the
simple truth the bible says bears a

resemblance to paradise on earth.

The Park

one Friday night with
pounding hearts, in the
weak dark of the streets
holding hidden injuries,
with the airy chatter of
the Pentecostals exiting
a roomy storefront spot
frequented for song and
prayer, we walked uptown
to the great fountain, where
the musicians without names
mingled with lovers holding
hands, the laughing Puerto
Rican girls dressed in white,
and the boys close by them
sipping drinks on slanted park
benches. we sat watchfully
before sweet gasps of love
followed!

Witness

when I was born the streets
shouted the name of a women

named Rosa Parks who refused
a bus driver's order to give up

her seat to a pale faced rider,
they spoke Spanish in the alleys

about a man named Martin Luther
King, Jr who within days took up

the serious business of planning
a march with citizens to gain

justice on the bus, Malcolm X
became the minister of Temple

Twelve in the city that loves you
back, massive Puerto Rican migration

to big cities went into full swing, and
within a few years Cha-Cha Jimenez

founded the Young Lords inspired
by reading The Seven Story Mountain

penned by a monk, and stories of Martin,
Malcolm and Black Panthers' calls for

self-defense. I grew up hearing a song
boom on the block, deep in my heart, I

do believe we shall overcome some day,
and in the library each day hung out with

Langston Hughes, James Baldwin, Piri
Thomas and Pedro Albizu to find out why

America called us spics. I hurried off
to school each day tears streaming down

my brown cheeks, learned nothing about
people like me, trafficked Spanglish on the

playgrounds telling brown faces teachers
have no idea we belong and the priests up

the street in the corner church deny at the
Last Supper not one white face was at the

table to taste Christ bread. after many years,
I still hear stories that keep me believing we

shall overcome someday!

A New Song

God was barely listening
to the streets today with

all the noise being made
at church. in deafening

voices they prayed, read
words with the whistling

wind at the front door, the
pews filled with stunned

looking eyes and wide open
ears to hear the story of the

teen unwed mother the Angel
said with child. Lord, have

mercy for the neglected ones
who roam the nights where

you happen not to be. heaven
has other designs for earth

the true believers declared
weeping for the One born

with wounds nesting on his
infant flesh, and the worn faces

of beggars that never enter the
church at the nearest corner

were like always questioning
the Glorious One said full of

love and care. Lord, have mercy
on the forgotten when you rest

in warm rooms, quickly rise to
met them on the streets, take them

by their cracked hands, remove
the anger from their trembling

bones and remember you said
the meek will inherit the earth.

Lord, come down to our streets
right now and stand beside those

who bleed.

The Season

I often wonder about how many
tears are shed when trying to make
sense of the expensive politics
planting crosses on the side of
the road to keep company some
day with the towered wall planned
with large indifferent walks. little is
ever said of Bethlehem happening
in these parts, the wrenching hate
spilling from so many tongues, the
citizens lurking in the dark believing
the divine illuminating day and night
does not see. I often wonder about
the meek of the earth knocking on
the door in tears who are misjudged,
why the lovely carols we sing pass
overhead the citizens white flesh, and
why so much godly chanting rarely
delivers peaceful dreams to the innocent
outside the gate. tell me will the lowly
truly rise or Herod's kin lay hope to
final rest? tell me, how many fires
will be made today to commit the good
book to flames? will the mighty work
be done? tell me, what is next?

The Café

come night on the lower east side,
on the quiet side of the bar, he sits

alone writing prayers with a warm
hand that has not slept for the last

forty years. he looks around the loud
room, glances with a smile at the soft

faces out that night in the Nuyorican
poets' café to speak countless things, the

murmuring of hamlets, rivers, mountains
and streets long left, the whistled longing

carried by their limbs and the salon singers
making them feel at home. he notices dust

dancing in stage lights, the brown eyed
girls moving their hips in step with the

house band, and the evening seems
entirely penetrated with the presence of

the Highest. his eyes again are fixed
on a notebook, the minor scale played

by a trombone on the other side of the
room lamenting beneath his skin, the

new made memories in the bar slowly
conjuring syllables on his pages, in language

conserving history, registering cultural highs
and planting signs to lead others to a valley

of peace, colorful gardens that grow
sweet wheat and the places love itself

was born—in that noisy room with its
dim light words do not appear to him

in vain.

Iron Cage

once I went to church to
find a little proof from on

high that brown people on
the block existed and they

would taste happiness on
their cracked lips. I looked

around the sanctuary like
a kid playing in a sandbox

at a cheap daycare center for
for the first time, wanted to

light a few candles but didn't
have a dime for the donation

expected, listened to the string
of prayers offered by priests who

never mentioned the low-income
kids, and waited for sleepy truth

to stir. I sat patiently hoping to
concretely grab a miracle or two

though it must have been the wrong
time of day for not one creeped into

the room, the mother next to me in
the same pew like Peter three times

denied the collection plate that came
by acting like an orphan with special

needs, and the old man sitting in front
of me winked with his most wrinkled

eye as if to say all is not lost. imagine
Sunday with a whole lot of brown people

backing out of bitterness in a tucked away
church, English, Spanish and Spanglish

words shouting directions to the land of
milk and honey nobody seems to find.

well, I went back the next week with fifty
more brown questions and the unbearable

feeling that centuries of complaining left
us in the dark.

The Stone

maybe the light coming
from the window will
touch us today long enough
to help us see the brown God
who causes panic in white churches.
maybe it will explain why we
grow up tugging at dreams filling
others with fear. we may even
have a few answers about why
the uptown world spends time
feeling troubled by us. when that
little light comes into the room
full of brown bodies, maybe light will
shine on a disfigured divine figure who
will appear speaking Spanish like us,
looking like the stranger who just moved
in to the apartment next door, standing
there like a mystery that does not make
us tremble, pouring words of aged truth
like wine no one can afford to buy. maybe
when the light delivers to us this brown
God talked about on the corners and the
back of the church, the all-day dark like
the old stone will simply roll away.

War

I followed the stars
to come to you in the
night, when the gun
fire was silent, and
your holy eyes were
shut in deep sleep.
you, my own dear,
were there for me to
look upon your face
the soldiers scarred,
but was no less bright.
I sat quietly in the dimly
lit room, on watch until
the face of dawn danced
on the civil war streets,
and in the grieving time
of this tiny country, I knew
we would never be severed
by soldiers, or the bloody
hours of this butchering civil
war.

Work

on the first page of
his notebook it reads
the beginning of the
journey to a foreign
land. once on the block
looking at the gutted
buildings, the coatless
bums, the pushers, junkies,
police chases, dark streets,
he wonders what he has
done. he walks up the street
passed the elementary
school, where the early
morning bell rings, the
corners of his pockets
empty to the touch, gets
to a 7/11 to shift from one
foot to another, waiting in
the creases of passing time
for work to find him.

Bethlehem

once
a year
children's eyes
grow big,
when they
imagine
what's inside
the wrappings
beneath trees.
homes fill with
seasonal song,
monks chant
their halls
with cheer,
and the road
to Bethlehem
is not ever
more
clear.
in the
small apartment
on the
second floor
a solitary candle
flames,
children
with too little
to eat
play games
they know
well, and a

mother
who prayed
heaven to
earth
offers love
boxed for
them with
a kiss.

The Miracle

through the falling snow
the buses rushing by the
only synagogue left on the
street, I saw the figure of
a poor old woman bent
over making her way across
the avenue, to the edge of
the sidewalk, where she
stood idle before raising
one foot over the curve.
she looked familiar to me
by the hunched shoulders,
the slow steps behind a two
wheeled grocery cart, her lips
talking with nobody, and the
look in her eyes announcing a
mind slowly flying away. for
years I had seen her, received
from her wrinkled hands strange
European sweets, and listened
to her tell delicious tales, when
I carried her groceries home. You
know, she is wiser than the good
book, a devout Jew in the South
Bronx, honey from heaven I first
met on the sidewalk a week before
the savior's birth—I must tell you
this old woman touched me more
than prayer.

Cathedral Steps

the stranger will visit
when night sits on the
Cathedral steps. his cool
brown face will peddle soft
calls to pedestrians out on
evening parade in exchange
for some simple change. he
will find a thousand different
ways to carve light from the
Fifth Avenue darkness, imagine
the Holy Mother frowning on the
world that runs away from his
smell, and shivering between the
big buildings speaking loud to himself
about the coming of the Prince of
Peace. giving thanks for the coins
dropped in his paper cup by a suited
man with a fancy hat, it won't be long
until a smile appears on his wind-sore lips
to disclose an inner thought—vain faith
never brims with heaven!

Not Far

I want to lie down on the
damp sand at Orchard Beach

with soft rain falling, to shut
my eyes on the old blanket

that rushed to the Bronx from
an island in the middle of a

vast sea, and remain at rest till
the dark circles about shouting

names. I want to walk down
the street in pouring rain making

stops along the way in front of
the abandoned building that laid

Joseph to rest, the sidewalk that
allowed Rudy a last breath, the

storefront where the hurt lifted
prayers, the stoop where Carmen

Julia graduated to the life of a dope
fiend and to the front steps of the

Cathedral where people praying are
overlooked. I want to walk held by

the hand of abuelitas' very own
guardian Angel toward light, and

when at the little park, see her
elegant figure leading us passed

wretched life. I want to lie down on
the sidewalk on Westchester Avenue,

till the clocks stop spinning, then
shout with a clear voice on the

block I know a few places
where truth rests.

Exile

the crowded houses on the
hill among the mango trees
with withered men, women
and children inside of them
are beginning to fade in the
distance. in hungry eyes you
see the exile has begun before
crossing the border into the land
where they carry homes in small bags.
what will they do cast out from
the place believed home? will they
learn English sooner than their kids,
or wait for Spanish letters mailed
from the villages with native tongues
begging them back? they are already
caught in spaces of remembrance,
accompanied by fear, uncertain
of the use of prayer, exhausted by
the absence of peace. identity for
them on the northern steeps is on
the run, their bodies anticipating
the crunching of bones that comes
at the hands of those who hate, and
life in a foreign land unbearable to
think—how long in exile will they
be confined and know rejection for
their lives?

The School

his mother had not been to
the school where her fourth

grade boy was learning to
name the world in English in

Mrs. Johnson's class, along
side of the names of presidents,

and the stabbing words making
him entirely invisible despite a

City Hospital birth just two blocks
up the street from the place. in the

soft early morning light, hanging
her head out the window the mother

shouted Nestor learn what you can,
don't believe the teachers who say

people like you don't belong in
America, and tell them you come

from corn old like the brown earth
now home to these United States. on

the school yard running with friends,
the boy smuggled Spanish into play

defying a teachers' language ban, then
after school, he walked home recalling

a book he checked out of the library by
Mark Twain titled *What* Stumped *the*

Bluejays, featuring talking animals. the
boy could not wait to read it to his mother

who knew about these magical worlds and
their colorful words.

Tax Reform

the poverty-stricken marchers
are up in arms today about the tax

plan voted in by politicians in finely
tailored suits who have given citizens

a future more contemptible than them.
who ever imagined chiselers, misfits,

hypocrites and crooks with spittle
bubbling on their lips would see their

cruelest will come true. what will glad
fools do when the lines circle about the

capital with citizens without means? what
will they do with the voices rising from the

ashes of the hellish political heads? What
excuses will they give for the uncountable

sorrow they have purchased for society with
dim witted ideas? What will they say when God

leans in to hear the people they have exiled
to bitterness? what will the sweet-mouthed

politicians say the day the sound of silver
coins rattling in their pockets leads them to

the horrid gates of hell?

Homeless

I entered the mission place
with its stacked high beds,

speechless in the prayer hall
where a uniformed soldier for

Christ shouted and I saw a
lighted room full of winos

among the quick, along with a
few runaway kids near dead. I

wondered quietly in the back of
the chapel about the indifference

of the citizens for God, those who
came to pray in this place for

crumbs. I never saw more outlawed
flesh in a single room than in the

mission house sharing doughnuts,
beds and prayers with stubborn bums

and lost kids. when the shouting from
the uniformed men stopped, we were

given a single sheet of paper with words
for our sore hearts to sing, which I had

never done in my old Catholic church.
I slept on a top bunk stacked five high,

a boy in a room full of acid tears, giving
my own thanks to the unknown for at

least one night off the street. I never
forget the wake-up call for the damned,

being shown the front door, the smiles
that said good day—God help us I

muttered on the sidewalk for
the helpless inching away.

Unto Us...

when the city blanketed
by snow is ignited at night
with lights and the church
bells ring to announce the
coming of the infant child
with a heart that beats with
gracious love for worldly
grief to flee, then we will
confess with bent knees the
lamb of God and prince of
peace among us. when the
homeless on the corner start
to sing beneath the shining
stars, and their arms are raised
in prayer, and eternal silence
with innocent sobbing begins to
speak, Gloria with Mother Mary
we shall together croon! when
the stench of the manger floats
about these streets, and Caspar,
Balthazar, Melchior are translated
to Spanish names, then the mystic
birth of the Word made flesh, el
Cristo from Belen will truth and
justice bring.

Departure

what does it feel like
when you put the letter
in an envelope, walk it
to the post office on 167th
Street, with long tales of
the places you visited in
New York that you first
saw in the photographs of
a book a thousand starlit
nights ago, beside the long
haired girl who shouts your
name from afar? why do
you set a plate for her each
morning before you head to
work in the metal shop when
the sky begins to take on the
same light that shines across
the border? why did you linger
in the shadowy hours of night
on the rooftop holding a candle
that danced in the gentle wind,
with your brown eyes wet like
the Rio Grande you crossed to
escape villainy and chains? you
said one watery evening that in
this new country you miss her
loveliness—now I understand.

The Box

his mother who lived
at the last stop of the

crosstown bus got sick.
the boy who came for

weekend visits tried in vain
to convince her to see a doc,

he talked to Santitos on a
dresser, lit a few candles

to them and begged for the
curse making his mother ill

to flee. by the hour, he checked
on her sitting beside the bed asking

the woman who spoke his name
beneath strained breath whether

or not his prayers to saints produced
a change in her illness. that night, he

sat turning the two-room apartment into
a prayer house, begging in holy silence

for a miracle to get to work on his mother's
lungs. he recycled every word from Santero

meetings and church, but the next day
not even Jesus helped his mother out

of bed. she began without warning the
journey to dust with fluid in her lungs,

days later the boy prayed beside a box
of cheap wood lowered into a South

Bronx grave, changed.

Redemption

a welfare reject roamed the
avenues collecting aluminum
cans for recycling in exchange
for a little change. he recalled
days rummaging bags with last night's
putrid remains from the apartments, the
long walks during holiday seasons on
the avenues lined with lovers and friends,
entering his favorite Cathedral on Fifth Avenue
to make confession, the kids who once
giggled at the English that issued from
his lips, the wife who escaped with another
lover before his last shot of dope entered
his aging veins. sometimes, early in the
morning, when Cathedral pews were
most empty, he would make a visit to
cry out to the miraculous One to disentangle
him from the Midnight Express clinging
to his liver and the dope complaining daily
in his veins for a fix. he reached for another
item inside a can on Loisaida Avenue, hope
hanging like a rosary around his neck, certain
a different hour full of grace and a whole
lot of mercy would trickle down for him.

The Infant

it is winter in the old place
whose floors are paced with
gentle steps by a mother with
an infant in her arms. she lets
her prayers roll into the three
rooms where Angels make visits
when she calls to them with
songs. you can see her at the
window preparing for things to
come in a world of hardship
and grace, joyfully whispering
in the newborn's ear the words
received from perfect dust that
peace for this foreign world is
near. in this apartment, there is
no need for certain knowledge
of heavenly things, nor proof
the babe is caressed by love, for
the saving story told by some, the
Mighty filling earthly lungs with
breath is joined to her poor flesh.
you can see her at the window inviting
you in, selling you the light she collected
from stars kept on an altar with Saints, tales
to open your ears and lead your eyes
to see new things—alleluia I adore
this mother's name!

Waiting

in the building there are
hundreds of doors with light

spreading around their edges,
people inside gathered about

candles on altars to talk with the
dead, throwing profanities at the

days giving little to eat, the holy
places dripping candles unable

to produce a world of peace, the
costly knowledge that Spanish

cannot speak, and the church bells
that naïvely ring. when the kids in

apartment 3B come out, they talk about
a father who has three years left to serve

and write his name with magic markers
on a lamp post in the middle of the block

they wish to make their amen spot. in this
barrio, the days slowly crawl for worn people

who trudge long days at work, send their kids
to crowded schools, and weep at night in bed

when the bill collectors knock. they wonder
does God even frown? in the corner grocery

store, where the old islanders play dominoes,
the people fed up with the Highest who is

charmed by their weaknesses, gather to
exhale for a few moments—do you see?

The Rescue

there is a church on the
block in what used to be
a beauty salon, the stylist

who cut hair in the place
is long gone, old men now
linger just outside its door

like outcasts, while inside
people with wishful eyes
make noise, sing and pray.

there is no sign above the
door that says its name, the
junkies on the corner next

to it sometimes say it has a
bit of light and once in a great
while they hear the preacher

shout from slavery we are set
free. an old woman paused to
look through a window covered

by a black curtain with a few see
through spots trusting her sweet
brown Lord understood why she

kept sabbath walking the early
morning streets. a couple of kids
exit to the sidewalk, they are busy

talking about a junior high school
they attend, St. John's where they
were baptized, and how they slipped

away unnoticed. on a wall beside
the storefront you can read painted
words that say weep dear God for

the poor—deliverance, please!

New Year

those
who somehow
found
a bit of truth
in spun lies,
tweeted tizzies,
inexcusable moral
indecency,
monstrous acts
of injury
and self
adoring lines
will run into
a future
with a scrap of
government
behind.
those filled
with
ignorant
compliance,
and occupied
with whitish
evangelical
muck, will
soon live the
same misery
as those they
deeply hate.
those who have
asked questions

say
if light
cannot
overcome
darkness,
what use
have we
of it!

The Bus

time was on the back of
the bus making its way

across the city passed the
sleepy buildings too old

to weep. the people began
to stir in apartments trying

to recollect the smell of mangoes
cut beneath the dancing leaves

of trees, the women gathering
water at a river's edge, the sounds

of the morning arranged like words
in the sky, and pigeons circling the

Cathedral where children once wiped
their noses on Romero's dusty robes.

at the bus stop their eyes stretched across
the long distance to see the mountains

scratching heaven for a cord longer than
Rapunzel's hair, the spot along the path

of humble stones where a few of them
buried a tiny cross to let earth in that far

away place remember them. the woman
with hands that beat the darkness held a

rosary pondering on the way to work taking
care of English only children what God thinks

about the wall, do we really begin with Adam
and Eve, and who listens to them walk in the

valley of bones. the bus finally arrived to pick
up the hardworking passengers the Black driver

knew by name and together they slipped away
to the next block.

The Sad Years

years from now stories
will be told by the children
who suffered, the greying
citizens with sad eyes, the
new Americans who bore
the nation's mistakes, and
the unpretentious people who
did not applaud the politicians
who legislated woe. they will
ask the writers of history what
the elected officials did to prevent
a spiteful president from taking
the nation to an absurdly closer
grave, what alternative facts will
justify democracy's shame, how will
they account for the departure of love,
the spread of injustice, the practices of
hate, and the millions magnified with
contempt? years from now we will begin
the stories of this time in tears, grandparents
will not take credit for what happened and
in misery many will confess the betrayal of
the nation's soul.

Come

I walked a few miles to
to see the river filled with
dreams and sat for hours
waiting for people to come
for a plunge. when evening
widened, I made a fire on its
shore lacking the desire then
to jump in and danced in the
flickering light with the shadows
moving on the gently curving
waters. I skipped rocks a few
times across the river surface,
stopping every so often to kneel
and take in the delicacy of that
summoning place. I could hear
voices arise from the whispering
flow of the current and feel the
unseen in the minutes coming to
to me delicately calling.

The Priest

they say Father Rossi was
fond of reading novels written

by South Americans at certain
times of the day to take his mind

to places beyond Hoe Avenue.
On Wednesday afternoon, when

kids were released for religious
instruction, they would often find

him reading Marquez delighting
in his way of depicting the intrusion

of the fantastical and magical in the
world. the aging priest familiar with

the suffering of the weak, the endless
daily struggle of the Spanglish speaking

Bronx, the triumph of corrupt politics,
the masses said for the young dead, the

prayers recited for the undocumented
in detention, the wailing widows, battered

mothers, abused children, intemperate men,
and the social ills contrived by greed, earned

the right to an escape. he often wished the
happiness restored by the words whose ink

grew a little fainter each week to tear a hole
into his corner of the world and like a swollen

river drench it with the uncovered treasures
of the good life waiting to be found in the

block's piled high dreams—that I suppose
is why he told us to find the precise truth

of things!

Manna

sometimes you walk down the street
looking for the man who sells sugar

cane from an old supermarket cart
with one wheel that never spins, or

you head to the grocery store owned
by the Puerto Rican family that lost

their youngest boy to a war to grab a
pastelito de carne, while observing old

ladies arriving at regular intervals to pick
up a container of juice from the freezer

and play two dollars on the numbers. on
the street, you remember little Papo was

stabbed after school in front of the church
Victor pushed by in his new wheelchair, you

shake your head once again hungering for a
time of peace. the sweet sound of music then

comes from the old-fashioned record shop,
the neighborhood wino is dancing for dimes

on the sidewalk, and you feel yourself drawn
closer to the aching block. sometimes those

who expect these brown people to simply
meet their end are disappointed, and we go

on to enjoy beneath the moon, sun and stars
the sweetest sounds of laughter made by those

who know manna will crack the sky and drip
into their open mouths.

Snapshot

when was it that I noticed
in a draw a black and white

photograph of children in
Catholic school dress and

you were among them. I
could not help staring at it

trying to figure what faces
were familiar to me. your

childish look with a bright
smile and partly covered on

one side with long hair held
my attention longer than I can

remember. the children were
carefully exercising a practiced

grin for the nun's camera even
with the civil war pounding on

the compound doors. I can tell
you that your smile has remained

unchanged, even when you close
your eyes to say to me one day I

will meet others in the photo of
that school. you should know I

started the new year in a church
lighting candles imploring Mother

Mary to turn your prayers into miracles
as you requested years ago, with hoarse

screams in the Spanish speaking Cathedral
of another country. perhaps, when I get home

tonight, I will ask the unseen God to
listen and tell you comfort is crawling

toward you holding a copy of the same
school yard picture and exciting darkness

until it exudes light around you.

Thought

we like sitting in the still of
morning waiting for the light
to enclose it, experiencing the
fainting moon in a bluing sky,
the feuding darkness curving
out of sight, the simplicity of
each breath slipping into a new
day to keep watch, and laughter
singing in soft wind. we like the
silence that explains nothing, the
mystery filling the earth, the wrinkling
passage of time whispering death is
not in charge of things, the countenance
of divinity making the rounds to close
quivering lips, and the nameless awe that
leans without a word into us.

Martin

you would not recognize me
on the streets in 1968 on the day
they killed Martin Luther King,
I was the homeless, strung-out
kid that soon after watched the
streets set on fire in Harlem and
the news with flames aiming to
devour hate. the faces appearing
at the window ledges on Lenox
Avenue were drenched with angry
tears, America could not imagine
equality for everyone and justice
across the land shunned dark skin.
precious Lord why don't you take
our hand was moaned by people on
the streets, gathered on the corners,
setting fires to car tires and throwing
things. I remember Mahalia singing
the hymn at the funeral of our beloved
Martin, Robert Kennedy reporting the
news begging us not to be devoured by
hate and reminding us a white man killed
his brother. nowadays I remember Martin
in my country that is far from his dream,
forgetful of our centuries of scars, and
letting the strong slowly devour the weak.
still, I believe Martin's dream will never
stop threatening the architects of loathing
with the vision from above of justice, equality
and peace for all!

Holy Spirit

even the thorns shed tears
when the splintered wood

for every eye to see called
through his cries disciples to

stand unafraid. the gallow-tree
with us still marvels at the way

we have made mercy, justice
and love a cozy living room

thing, the death of martyrs a
sung memory and the suffering

of the poor a day to pray up the
dust. dear Lord, we look away

from sickening pain, turn away
from Caiaphas' schemes, agree

with witless politicians who look
directly at the sun, and permit the

minutes to crawl not shouldering
the cross. sweet Christ, Martin,

Romero, Bonhoeffer, Ignacio, Segundo,
Ramon, Joaquin, Amando, Elba, Celina,

Jean, Dorothy, Ita, Maura, and all
trampled beings forgive our tidy

silence, break loose our chained tongues
and make us speak.

High Ground

darkness did not keep us
from walking the streets

with the olden stars lighting
the way. we passed the same

cracked brick tenements, faces
looking from windows, children

on the fire escapes taking in
the near absence of light, the

girls on their last game of hop
scotch who tenderly laughed

like they were uttering verse, the
old Jewish couple who placed

beach chairs on the sidewalk in
front of their stoop displaying

in their eyes the candles for years
burning inside them, the people

exiting the church where they fell
to their knees simply to confess once

more things buried inside them, and
arrived finally at an open field in Crotona

Park where the sights, sounds and smells
met us and dismissed the certain crucifixion

that chased us each day on the streets.

Dawn

beloved,
on the block from countries
of origin not publicly named, living
in the shadows, slowly withering away
as tyrants who tortured, falsely jailed
and killed adore exile in these United
States, hold on and never drown in your
tears.

beloved,
to those coming to you in the day light
saying, keep your foot off the door,
God is not near and your only freedom is
the right to die, stare straight back without
fear.

beloved,
waking in the middle of the night from the
unbearable things lunging into sleep from
the rock bottom of your wounded hearts, quiet
your screams, lift your heads and leave the
dawn to the understanding of the sweet border
crossing Lord beside you.

beloved,
you who labor hard each day to wish a
new life, who argue with silence in the
heavens, a thousand trumpets in this
multicolored America will sound and a
riotous throng will sing your names and
you will slip over the walls, drink from

justice springs and trample Golgotha's
bitter ground.

Passage

what is it like to know
your secrets forged in
the beginning my dear
ageless time? what is
it like never to be late,
to simply be there, to
accompany all things
and drink day after day
the substance of sweet
dreams? what is it like
to listen to us rejoice and
grieve in our swift flesh,
complain of severed love,
rattle our aging bones and
toss dizzying words at the
gates of heaven? when we
cry to you can you hear, do
you know the places where
gods listen, or are you ever
tired of clocks? time, you
will never know why I feel
satisfaction on a midnight
roof holding you in hand,
waiting.

No Safe Haven

last night sitting with friends about
to lose T.P.S., talking tearfully about

the humanitarian statute Congress
first passed twenty-eight years ago

to aid people unable to return home
given civil unrest, violence and earth

quakes, recalling George H. Bush
extended it to Salvadorans after the

murder of the Jesuits, their cook and
her daughter, then George W. Bush

and Barack Obama granted it to the
people of the tiniest country in Central

America so familiar with what it means
to live in the shadow of the United States

and her inescapable Good Friday, we
wept. Segundo remarked it is a good time

for us to scream Oscar Romero Ora pro nobis,
Sonia thought it was a sign for marching on

the streets in defense of the human
rights of the vulnerable, then everyone

sighed nowadays no one believes in justice
for the weak, and in truthful political speech,

just the architects of indifference who want
to make a lily White country with moves

to disappear us. then, we sat quietly for a long
time, a candle in a glass covered with the image

of Mother Mary burned on the table night flickering
in the dim light, we experienced the country tumbling

deeper into hate!

Get Out!

she tried not to remember the
stony street that ran the length

of the stream to which voices
in the Colonia clung making

words only intelligible to the
people occupying the mansion

in the sky. after all these years
in the North, she clearly hears

the sound of the bells from her
school near the Cathedral that on

still nights cries for her murdered
Archbishop, sees flowers carefully

arranged in the graveyard where
the prematurely dead were laid in

plots with hardly visible stones and
clumsily etched names, recalls wiry

soldiers who made the rivers in the
country turn red, and the women of

the market place with their young
who worked seven days a week until

their bones dried up. she taught school
among the poor who were blamed by

the governors for scars they inflicted,
trampled by hatred inspired by greed,

and swallowed by the earth beneath the
oligarchy's feet. soon, she will move out

of her overcrowded room, stop taking
care of the white children in her keep,

pack her rosary without cures in a small
bag with clothes, walk the streets of the

city a last time, and hear stinging voices
at the border in unison yelling the cold

and inhospitable words: Get out!

The Border

they crossed the border in
their heads for months before

seeing it that night for the
first time, no border patrol,

no obstacles, no citizens in
America to throw them

back to villages where flies
darken the sky with death.

children held tightly by the
hand asked is heaven holding

in her arms a new life for us
in that place, mothers looked

back at the old country they left
weeping, yes. they shared the moon,

stars, sun, water and air with people
on the other side who stutter at the sight

of their brown bodies, accented speech
and belly full of dreams. they carry bags

filled with tiny crosses to help tear down
the thick walls, spend hours practicing the

funny sounding English words to find
their way on crowded streets to the old

tenements with a mattress to call home
and to make sense of the anti-Latino rants

broadcast on English only radio. after
crossing, they will work stacking dishes,

cleaning houses, sweeping floors, cutting
grass, harvesting crops, in the factories

and tending well-to-do white kids. they

will visit church less often, sob awake
at night, hug their innocent niños, get

rounded up by ICE, and be forced across
the border again to face the violence of

gangs born in Los Angeles, Chicago and
the New York streets—when will the

world say enough?

El Salvador

in the morning rush
with a light rain falling

on the rooftop, the long
walk with the warming

sun to the top of the hill
to the small church with

wood carved saints slips
into me. I can hear the

bell tolling in the distance,
the steeple casting a long

shadow on the street, the
brown earth on the side of

the road pounded by elderly
women dressed with black

scarves on their heads on the
way to sell cheap things at

the local market and speeding
along to make a Mass that

offers life. when I reach the
hill top, a flock with holy names

gathers on the sidewalk to hear
the grey priest speak charmed

words that makes women sing into
God's ears. when the time is

right, I enter the sanctuary with
the crippled, poor and bent from

the Colonia tossing inside of me,
walk directly to the altar of our Lady

of Peace, speak to her about the near
dead and look into her down-cast eyes

to plead deliverance for my slum.

Paradise

in simpler times the nights
gave way to humble silence,

flowers were tossed around
in our talking dreams, stars

above us enchanted the dark
streets, children quietly rested

on their mothers' knees and
heavenly winds visited us in

old tenements we called, home.
our weeping, laughter, family,

and friends shared stories each
day to keep our hearts complete

and many distant voices whispered
to us in the dark that paradise is waiting

on the next corner. tonight, look into
the insisting eyes, gently touch the

scathed strangers' souls, and tell
us when will you return to give

us peace?

Holy

what is the day for when it
wakes you from wherever
you had been in sleep? will
you wander the city searching
the crowds with your eyes for
someone seen in a dream? will
you stand on Avenue B trying
to hear the sea beating against
Salvadoran shores, listen for
voices unfolding in the morning
like love, and watch the climbing
sun heave shadows down the long
street? how many steps will you take
to find the hands that hold you and
keep your secrets? how many prayers
will your mind raise for a God who
forgets to relish your sweet breath
and hear your cries for daily bread?
permit me to keep you company until
the evening falls or we find the stones
that speak.

The Word

the uneven sidewalk led me
to a collection of cracked bricks
on the side of the city with old
buildings where the dark inside
was lit with candles that burned
in crowded rooms. I could hear
the stoops as the night fell on the
streets panting without enough air
for the block and people on the steps
hollering about their strung-out days
in a country going out of its way to
devour them. I passed Lazarus who
was nodding out on a milk crate in
front of the Perez bodega unashamed
of his sores, bumped into Rosario who
argued the week before in the storefront
church must there be death for people
like us before resurrection, found myself
thinking how strange it is to believe, and
questioned what time of day would the
kids we put in the ground rise. I reached
my decaying tenement making it to its
moonlit rooftop, found a small group of
grandmothers on it restoring hope with
Spanish words of praise, so I clinged to
them beneath the all-knowing stars and
let my reticent tongue pray.

Hold My Hand

I began life on this block
when the pushcarts still carried
stalks of sugar cane from the boat
yards to the mouths of the Puerto
Rican kids, in this old neighborhood
where Patron Saint processions marched
in the broken bottle alleys, paused on
the junkie stoops and coughed up prayers
to sickly faces. We read the Spanish
papers that were used by the local wino
like a bed sheet in a stairwell in Flaco's
building, roamed the local creek like
wandering widows dressed in black
for permanent Via Crucis, and went to
schools to read all the stories of people
who never looked, talked or breathed
like our beautiful brown kin. I walked
past the big Catholic church everyday
on the way to buy dope for my scrawny
adolescent veins, made the sign of the
cross along the way, kept one step ahead
of Tarzan's knife, and wondered when the
Angelic train would come along whistling us
aboard. I saw the old tenement's bricks come
tumbling down, people left no place to call
home, sat with my late brother in the middle
of one lot to remember the slow joys of an
old apartment, and cried one last time with
him for the wide heavens to speak. tell me
what shall we say to the next generation,
what comfort can we offer their tremulous

days, and how long before they see milk
and honey spread out for them?

Dark Space

evening rolled over us
clearing what remained
of a long day washing dishes
in a hotel kitchen, a light drizzle
misted the air like Holy water
from the River Jordan sent to
cleanse the great crowd exiting
the subway station, absorbed by
Spanglish talk of an unreadable
God. each step closer to the crowded
room called home liberated us from
fear, and delivered us to a world
unreached by the Department of
Homeland Security and its cold
detention cells. they will never stone
us on these forsaken streets, and in the
coming future we will hook them with
light!

Politics

I have thought too long of
politics in the upper rooms

with splintered tables, where
we listen to broken truths that

find their way to the pens that
stain paper with words to make

us fear. I have seen two-faced
politicians with whom Marquez

would surely parry, scan crowds
in their capital chamber skipping

over Brown faces, limping with
artificial knees to the podium to

take a stand of all things against
the kindness prayed for in far too

many blue-collar neighborhoods.
I see the poor still sleeping on the

tenement steps, pelted with Judas
kisses blown to them by a president

who turns away when their Black
and Brown bodies are dragged to the

hanging tree. I am too often lost
for words in the great valley of dry

bones where many sit in silence to
watch the perfect destruction of one

nation, indivisible! what will it be
like when life is transferred to the

waiting coffins with no one left to
sing America, America God shed

grace on thee?

Romero

see me in the Cathedral
the doors open wide for

the poor, the widows, the
orphaned, the hungry, the

tortured, raped, troubled
and reborn. I am the voice

crying in the wilderness, the
brown face of peasants who

shout in prayer God is not
dead, a revolutionary of a

Palestinian unwaged Jew long
ago lynched, a humble servant

of a future not my own, the
trembling voice of murdered

children, the tears of kidnapped
infants sold, the martyr of tens

of thousands of Christians, nuns,
pastors and priests pushed into

graves. I am bread, body and
blood, the naked truth of cities,

villages, and streets thirsty for
mercy, justice and love. I am

the government's subversive,
the most recent among crucified

slaves, the planter of peace, and
the prophet never silenced. I am

the broken body of my people,
the trodden longing to live free,

Oscar Romero!

March for Our Lives

the gun shots in schools let
loose by the errant hands of

those who will never weep
the innocent dead, oblivious

to the foul ill that feds now
on all the sorrowing hearts,

mocking the tears that collect
like dew in the hallways of so

many schools, still ring loudly
in us. the weekly gun violence

in America that makes death a
companion of teachers and kids,

the fierce wounds, the parents'
utter grief, and siblings visible

aches, no single round of prayer
can ease. the sweetest singers in

the funeral homes do their best with
weak voices to bring us close to

heaven's light, but our raging hearts
cannot let go of the awful wrong, and

they too will sink deep beneath the
graveyard earth. again and again the

politicians take the stage to name gun
violence tragic, the senseless acts of

the mentally deranged, but never once
the fault of their days in gilded halls

declining to do something about the
evil stain. who will mourn with us?

who will pace the stony road with
us until action ends this madness with

clear cut law? who will march for lives
until paradise comes near to fill us with

life again and confident peace?

Cone

he died after a noble life
surrounded by foes with

not a single breath taken
in vain. the whispering in

the church halls made by
those too close to revolting

rabid packs circling the lynching
trees and delivering a thousand

blows could never keep him from
answering with truth flowing like

a righteous river with crucified
blood. today, he more deeply sinks

into our hearts with words that
give us strength against a ghastly

culture of hate. now, sacred dark
feet trod the wretched stony roads

in tears beneath heaven that bid
him home and with weary steps

his beloved promise not to tire!
today, we search the skies with

his wondrous faith for the chariots
that huddle together to steal us away

from death and deliver us to the good
news in the blackness of a Crucified

God.

www.ingramcontent.com/pod-product-compliance
Lightning Source LLC
Chambersburg PA
CBHW062036220426
43662CB00010B/1521